YOU CAN TEACH

Young Teens

NORMA FELSKE

Updated, expanded from *Teaching that Grabs Young Teens*

Helps for Teachers
and Superintendents

VICTOR BOOKS
a division of SP Publications, Inc.
WHEATON. ILLINOIS 60187

Offices also in Fullerton, California • Whitby, Ontario, Canada • Amersham-on-the-Hill, Bucks, England

Bible quotations used in this book are from the *New American Standard Bible* (NASB), © by Lockman Foundation, La Habra, Calif.; the *New International Version: New Testament* (NIV), © 1973 by the New York Bible Society International; and *The New Testament in Modern English* (PH) © by J. B. Phillips, 1958, The Macmillan Company. All quotations used by permission.

VICTOR BOOKS
A division of SP Publications, Inc.
P.O. Box 1825 • Wheaton, Ill. 60187

ISBN: 0-88207-146-7
© 1981 by SP Publications, Inc. All rights reserved
Printed in the United States of America

Contents

Focusing on young teens
1

Hi! I'm a young teen (12, 13, or 14 years old). When I was younger, I could hardly wait till I started going to junior high (or middle) school. Now that I'm here, I'm pretty excited about all that is happening around me. My whole life seems to have changed a lot in the last few months. I'd like to tell you about me and my friends, so we'll understand each other. Of course, you already know something about what young teens are like—after all, you were one once. But a lot has changed since then. Only a young teen *now* can really know what it's like being a teen in today's world. So let me help you feel as I feel and see life as I see it.

I'm going through tremendous physical changes. Sometimes the rapid changes inside my body frighten me. I experience puberty at least a year earlier than young teens did just 15 or so years ago. I'm anxious and uncertain about my sexuality; but I try to hide my feelings with an air of sophistication. Some things I see on TV or in movies and read about in books make me think about male/female relationships that I don't have the skill or maturity to deal with. I need help in learning how to use my God-given sexuality in right ways.

My body is a big concern to me. It's not nearly as attractive or well-coordinated as I'd like it to be. I wish I could change some parts of it, or at least control them more! (At times I am really "klutzy"—

especially when I have to go in front of the class to give a report.) *My emotions vary and change quickly.* Sometimes I'm as surprised as anyone at the way I act. One time my feelings explode out of me, and another time I feel that I can't share what I feel with anyone, so I bury my feelings deep inside. Often I know I should apologize for things I've said or done impulsively, such as telling my mother I "hate" everything she wears; or talking back to Dad when he tells me to do some work around the house; or yelling at my brother when he messes up my room. But it's hard for me to express what I really feel, especially to members of my family.

I am searching for my own identity and want to explore my world. For the first time, I'm beginning to see myself as a person, rather than thinking of myself in terms of what I can or can't do. All kinds of confusing thoughts are starting to fill my head: Who am I? Where do I stand? What kind of man or woman should I become? (The kind my parents want me to be—or the kind society is telling me to be?) What is acceptable behavior? What personality traits are the most desirable? What life goals are important? Should I follow my parents' model, or should I "do my own thing"?

What values should I choose? Do my parents' values still make sense in today's world? I see such conflicting moral standards among the members of the older generation, I really wonder, "What is right, and what is wrong?"

Growing up isn't easy—no matter what adults may say. The pressures I feel inside and around me are great. Do you remember the things you did, just to see how far you could go, to say to the world, "Look at me—I'm a person"? You probably balked at going to church, or soaped windows, or maybe even got into a little bit of trouble with the law. I may do some of those same things, follow the latest fads for dress, or go with friends my parents don't approve of— even try drugs—to try to satisfy the need I have of finding out who I am.

I have a strong drive to be independent. I want more privacy now, time to think my own thoughts and dream my dreams. I seek more freedom from my parents, but at the same time, I really depend on them. They sometimes think, because I appear distant or withdrawn, that I don't love them. Teachers and other adult friends get the impression that I don't want their friendship. But this isn't true. I still want warmth and closeness with adults, and with all the members of my family, but in a different way than I did when I was a "child."

I have very real fears and worries. This may surprise many adults, but it's true. I worry about being accepted by the other kids at school, making good grades, or making the team. I fear such things as my parents getting divorced, my dad losing his job, our family moving to a new town, or getting killed in a car crash—even all of us getting wiped out in a nuclear blast! Almost anything an adult worries about, I can worry about—besides all the problems of growing up!

My view of the world is being shaped by TV. Though studies take up more of my time than they did when I was younger, I still have plenty of time to watch TV. For me and many of my friends, it is our favorite leisure-time activity. By the time I reach college age, I will have watched an average of 18,000 hours of TV. Both programs and commercials are greatly influencing my values, as well as giving me the opportunity to be passively involved in the world around me. TV is making me *aware.* I am constantly exposed to a barrage of news about world tensions, space programs, and social issues, as well as a sound explosion of all the current hit recordings. Have you ever watched TV through the eyes of a young teen? If I watch TV every day, what do you think my view of the world is?

I want to be accepted by my peers, but also by teachers and other adults. My friends are most important to me. They give me the understanding I need when I feel lonely and separated from my parents in the confusing process of growing up. When my parents' opinions about what I should do conflict with what my friends say, I frequently choose to follow my friends. I want so much to be approved by them that I dress, talk, and act as much like them as possible. *"Everybody* will be there!" and *"Everybody* has one!" are pleas I often use on my parents when I want to join the crowd in some activity, or buy something that the in-group is wearing. Standing out, or being thought of as "different" from the rest of the kids is one of the hardest things to face. So I really work at "fitting in."

My friends are not the only ones who are important to me, though.

Adults who make me feel that I matter, who care about me, and who listen to me share my thoughts and experiences without judging are high on my list of "neat" people.

I am full of questions, wanting to know why, and to understand the reasoning for many things. This is what teachers and parents want me to be able to do—to think for myself and take more responsibility for my own behavior. But when I challenge beliefs or values that they take for granted, they often can't cope. When I express doubts about Christianity, they really get uptight! They shouldn't be shocked, though. This is just my way of thinking through what I was taught as a child, and working out a genuine faith of my own.

I am fun-loving, enthusiastic, and energetic. Maybe this is why one youth leader said about me and my friends, "You've sure got to keep ahead of those kids every minute!" I like to *do* things, especially with a group of my friends. If you need help at a pancake breakfast, carwash, or senior citizens' craft night, we're the ones to ask!

We have our own kind of humor, and laugh at things that adults may think are silly or irreverent. And lots of their humor isn't funny to us.

I may not automatically respect adults and other authority figures. This may be the hardest attitude for you to deal with as my teacher. You were probably taught to respect your teachers and other adults, to listen to them, obey without question, and not talk back. But some of the trends in our school systems have taught me to react independently to information I hear. So I may question everything and everyone (including parents and Sunday School teachers). An adult's age or position won't automatically gain him my respect; rather, I may feel that he should first prove that he deserves it.

This lack of respect for authority and established institutions I may show can carry over into my attitudes toward the Bible and the kind of dress and behavior adults think is desirable in church. Teachers who expect me to come to Sunday School and church ready to listen to the Bible and accept it without question may be disappointed.

Generally, I am not as interested in formal religion as I used to be. I used to like to do my Sunday School lessons, learn verses, and be "good" in class to please my teacher or win my parents' approval.

Now, being thought of as religious or reverent is not important unless, of course, my friends are. Then I will probably conform to the way they behave. Generally, though, I am less interested in all the religious activities that the church plans for me than I used to be when I was a junior. I especially don't like to feel that I am being "preached at."

Well—there you have it, a picture of me in an exciting, but frustrating period of my life. I hope that what I have told you has helped you see that I am more than just a soul; I am a whole person—with real physical, emotional, and spiritual needs that I will satisfy in one way or another. Will you remember this, as you teach me and my friends?

We are all alike in so many ways; yet each of us is a special individual, different from the others. Discovering our uniqueness and relating to each one of us as a friend will be the challenge you face in teaching us young teens!

Make it yours
1. List as many characteristics of young teens as you can.
2. Think of the young teens you know. Write their initials next to the characteristics that are true of them.
3. What do you like best about young teens? Least? Ask God to give you a positive approach toward teaching this unique and challenging age-group.

Seeing your role as a teacher-guide 2

Young teens present as great a challenge as any other age-group in the Sunday School. How do you communicate with them? Do you have to dress as they do, adopt their casual way of grooming, follow their fads, and talk their language? Do you have to be under 30?

If these were the criteria, most teachers of young teens would flunk.

A thoughtful look at all the different kinds of people God is using to minister to this age-group tells us that teachers can understand and relate to the younger generation without trying to become members of it.

An effective teacher
What, then, are the qualities you need to be an effective teacher of young teens?

- You must have a practical working knowledge of God's Word and a living faith in Jesus Christ that you can express to young teens.
- You must be able to help young teens see how the Word of God relates to their personal problems and needs.
- You must be led, or "called," by the Holy Spirit to become a spiritual guide to these young people through what may be some of the most difficult years in their lives.

10

- You must be willing to work at building with them a relationship of acceptance, openness, and caring.
- You must have a flexible personality to withstand young teens' emotional immaturity.

Are you committed to teaching God's Word?

Any lasting ministry to teens must be centered in the Word of God, because:

1. *Young teens need to be saved from their sins, and they can't be saved apart from discovering what God's Word says, believing it, and applying the Scriptures to their own hearts' needs.* The Bible says, "Faith comes by hearing, and hearing by the Word of Christ" (Rom. 10:17, NASB). It is the Word that the Holy Spirit uses to bring about spiritual regeneration (James 1:18).

Many junior highs who have grown up in Christian families and can "speak the language" have never really been converted. They need to have many opportunities to reexamine what they have been taught, as well as what the Scriptures say about salvation, and make sure that they have a faith of their own.

You may also have in your class young people who have not had opportunities to hear and respond to the Gospel. Making the way of salvation clear and leading unconverted students to Christ should be the basic aim underlying all your teaching.

2. *Young teens need to know God, His will, and His ways.* God primarily reveals Himself through His Word. In the Bible young teens (who are looking for direction) can find the perfect plan He has for their lives and know the joy and security of fitting in with His purposes in creating them (Col. 1:9-10).

3. *Young teens need to grow and mature spiritually, learning to relate to other Christians and unbelievers in Christlike ways.* Teens can't grow without learning to feed on the milk and meat of the Word (1 Peter 2:2). "All Scripture is inspired by God and is useful for teaching the faith and correcting error, for resetting the direction of a man's life and training him in good living. The Scriptures are the comprehensive equipment of the man of God, and fit him fully for all branches of his work" (2 Tim. 3:16-17, PH).

4. *Young teens need God's wisdom, guidance, and strength to overcome the pressures, problems, and temptations that crowd their lives.* As they learn to pray and study and meditate on the Word, the Lord will enable them to stand and to learn by experience that He is a powerful, loving, and personal God (Ps. 119:105, 133).

5. *Young teens need to learn to accept themselves as individuals of worth.* In God's Word they find the basis for this—that they were created in the image of God (Gen. 1—3; Ps. 8) and redeemed by His Son (Titus 2:14).

6. *Young teens need a sense of belonging and acceptance.* In the Scriptures they discover what Christ's Church is, and learn that as believers they are important parts of the Body of Christ with other believers (Matt. 16:18; Acts 1—10).

7. *Young teens need something solid on which to base their values.* In the absolute, unchanging principles of the Word of God, teens find a sure foundation (Ps. 119:89; Matt. 5:18).

8. *Young teens need to have a sense of purpose for their lives.* They find this in responding to Christ's command to be personal witnesses for Him (Matt. 28:19-20; 2 Cor. 5).

But as excited as you may be about teaching young teens the Word of God, you don't always find them as motivated to learn as you are to teach. They are largely occupied with discovering their own identities and are taken up with the happenings in their own world of youth. To put the "want to" for Bible study into your students, and successfully guide them in their spiritual development, you must work at building with them a relationship of acceptance, openness, and caring. This involves time and energy.

Do you like teens?

A simple way to begin is by showing that you like teens and are enthusiastic about teaching them. Young people, in many instances, have a general feeling that adults disapprove of them. It's not hard to understand why they feel this way. Have you ever watched what happens when a group of noisy, happy teenagers climbs aboard a bus for a ride home from school, or perhaps a shopping trip on a free day? You can almost see some adults draw in their feet and their parcels, expecting the worst. Or notice how some adults react when a group of unchaperoned young teens "invades" the church balcony on Sunday night. Before they even get their coats off, some adults sitting nearby are throwing warning looks in their direction because they just *know* "those kids are going to act up and disturb the whole service!"

Even in the young teen department of the Sunday School, teachers may unconsciously show that they don't really like teenagers, but have taken on the responsibility of teaching them out of a sense of duty. Some teachers gather into groups before Sunday School begins and talk with each other on an entirely adult level, ignoring the young people to whom they are supposed to be ministering. Often the adults stay together at the back of the room until it is time for all of them to go to their classes. Only then do they talk directly with their students.

What does this kind of treatment say to young teens? They are highly sensitive to what older people think of them and quickly pick up adults' real feelings. In only one class session your students can learn a great deal about your attitude toward them.

Can you identify with them?

That you like young people and care about them will be clear to your teens as you begin to identify with them—first as a group and then as individuals. Their interests, needs, feelings, ambitions, and problems will become important to you. You will tune in to their world, becoming familiar with the kind of music they like, programs they watch on TV, their gripes and frustrations, and sharing with them in their fun and activities.

Building friendships with the persons in your class will take time, but it will bring great rewards; you will learn to love and appreciate each person as the unique individual God has made him. Visiting in teens' homes to meet their parents and see the kids in their activities away from Sunday School will give you revealing insights into how to relate your teaching to personal needs.

Whenever you are with the kids, on Sunday mornings or during the week, it is important to listen to what they say, without criticizing, letting them express what their problems are and what their lives are like. When they talk about their parents, you can help them understand the older generation. (And when you are with the "older generation," always keep your teens' confidences as you try to help parents understand their young people's needs.) By thus identifying with your teens, you will gain their respect and trust. You may not feel that you are successful in building a friendship with every teen, but it is important to keep making an effort. Having an open relationship with a young person is essential before you can begin to guide him spiritually.

A good example of a vital caring-sharing relationship is expressed in this teacher's description of her experiences with one of her students.

"Bobbi began attending our Sunday School early one summer. At first she was like a fish out of water. The sixth child in a family of 11 children, she was forced to come to church by her newly converted parents. Bobbi attended a 'rougher' junior high school than did the other girls in the class, and her family's social-economic status was considerably lower than the others'. But she gained admittance into the peer group rather easily. Those moments when she was isolated usually resulted from her choice to be aloof or withdrawn.

"Bobbi was painfully lacking in general Bible knowledge. She had many misconceptions and a distorted view of Scripture. Her feelings about going to church and learning from God's Word were probably typical of most young teens, yet Bobbi's reactions seemed more pronounced. She would usually listen and participate in our class discussions, and with the help of a modern translation she could answer factual questions and think through some concepts presented in a passage. Yet she never pretended to like being in church, and made it clear that the only reason she was there was that her parents made her come. Once in a while Bobbi was disruptive in the worship service or class; yet these times were directly related to times of intense inner turmoil.

"During the course of the year I had Bobbi as a student, I phoned her to remind her to bring back her manual, to tell her we missed her when she was absent, or just to talk. At these moments I sensed more 'adult' in her than at other times. She attended most of the out-of-class activities we had—bowling, softball games, going to McDonald's.

"Her home was right on the way to the softball field, so I often stopped by on the way to a church game. (By this time their phone had been disconnected.) She came once or twice even when there were no other junior highers in the car, which really surprised me because most of the girls in the class traveled only in pairs or trios. I think Bobbi was in some ways a little more mature for her age, perhaps because of the responsibility she had in her home. One time when she stayed overnight in my home, she offered to set the table for breakfast and then did it efficiently—watched the bacon while it cooked . . . poured the juice—quite in contrast to her junior high friend with her, who talked the whole time and generally was in the way.

"Though Bobbi was an intelligent girl, likable, and usually cooperative, she was sharp with criticism and quick with questions. Seldom did she wait for answers. Often there were no easy answers. She admitted to me one night when she and a friend were babysitting that she really could not believe deep-down there is a God. 'How can you say there is a God? If there is, why hasn't He answered my mother's prayers that my dad would stop drinking? All my life I've heard her ask God to make Dad stay sober, yet last night he was more bombed than ever! The new church kick he's on won't last. I just can't believe there's a God, or that He cares about my mom.'

"A few months later when Bobbi's six-year-old sister was severely burned in a kitchen fire, our church family prayed for and with the family for several weeks before the little girl died. Again Bobbi's question surfaced: 'If there is a God, how could He let Michelle die? All the people in the church were praying!'

"I have no idea how many of the words she heard that I or anyone else said. I suspect that two years from now she won't remember the great insights we may have shared with her. My guess is that if she remembers anything at all, it'll be the love expressed by the people who cared. That may someday be the propelling force which drives her to God."

Can you share with them?

As you identify with your teens, they will in time begin to identify with you—listening to you, accepting your teaching and advice, and modeling their beliefs and attitudes after yours. This is why it is so important for you to have a living, growing faith in Jesus Christ and to be honestly what you are before the members of your class. You needn't try to make them feel that you are perfect, for of course you aren't. But it is important to be honest and open with them, sharing some of the real struggles you have as you live the Christian life, and showing them how God meets your needs and helps you be victorious. Young teens need to see Christian living as it really is, not an unreal pattern of life without fears and frustrations, trials and temptations, weaknesses and failures. Sharing with them your own struggles (as well as your joys) will not cause you to lose respect in their eyes, but to gain respect. They will learn that they can be, as you are, in daily touch with God, and that the principles in His Word can be guiding lights for their paths through life, as they are through yours.

Can you "keep your cool"?

As you work to build relationships with your teens you will need to be flexible. Flexibility includes being realistic about what to expect from junior highs, allowing for their mistakes, and being able to adapt to the way they are.

Knowing that young teens are emotionally immature, you can expect behavioral problems to occur and avoid being shocked, angry, or hurt. For instance, because these young adolescents are impulsive and unpredictable, they may not respond to you one Sunday as they did the week before. A person with whom you have felt a special closeness may suddenly act as if he does not even like you. Will you react to him in the same manner in which he is treating you? Not if you love him and care about being able to guide his spiritual development. "Love is patient, love is kind" (1 Cor. 13:4, NIV). Your maturity should enable you to absorb your teens' ups and downs and keep moving toward your goals.

The better your teens get to know you and trust you, the more difficult it may be for you to restrain them in their actions. They will feel free to express to you any anger or resentment they may feel toward their parents or other adults, as well as their frustrations about their own inadequacies and failures. You will be wise to listen to them, without judging, and try to understand why they feel as they do. Regardless of how they act, they need to feel that you are their friend, that you think they are nice and accept them as they are.

At times, you will need to blend resiliency with firmness in letting your group know that you are the leader, with authority, in your class. They are capable of some responsibility, but are not adults. You will have to be the one to set bounds for them, letting them know clearly how far they can go. They may protest certain rules or restrictions you feel are necessary; but they usually feel happier and more secure when they know their limits.

What will you do when they break the rules and go beyond the limits? At times they will do this, for young teens can be buggable: They may upset programs, damage songbooks, write graffiti on furniture—even boycott the class of an unfavorite teacher. You will have to exercise discipline in a mature manner, one that will prevent offenses from becoming more serious than they really are. In each case, temper your discipline by regarding each student as a person worthy of respect, encouragement, and love.

> Father, I have shared my faith with them—
> These teens whom You have entrusted to me.
> They have seen me on good days and
>   bad days,
> Because they have shared my life.
> They have watched my reactions in
>   happiness and disappointment,
> And they know pretty much how I feel
>   about the issues of today.
> Because my relationship with You affects
>   everything else in my life,
> I have tried to be honest with You and
>   with them.

I loom large on their horizon this year
Because I am their teacher—confidant of
   some
And an accepted member of our class by all.
But this year will soon pass,
And with it the memory of what we have
   said to each other,
Of the things we've done together,
The plans we've made; the projects we've
   seen through.
And what will remain?
Please, Lord, let them feel that we have
   touched base with each other,
That our relationship can be picked up again
   when they need it.
But most of all, let them realize that their
   relationship with You
Is a living, growing one that will go on
   forever.
And may their sharing of themselves with
   others
Always grow out of their love-relationship
   with You.

                                    —E. Nicholson

Make it yours

1. What are five important qualities a teacher of young teens should have?
2. Why must a lasting ministry to young teens be centered in God's Word?
3. How can a teacher help put the "want to" for Bible study into his students?
4. Apply the phrase "What you do speaks so loud, I can't hear what you say" to your teaching situation:
    a. What do your actions in class say to your teens?
    b. What does the amount of time you spend with your teens outside class say to them?
    c. What effort are you putting into building personal relationships with your students?

Aiming for student response
3

INTERVIEWER: How long have you been serving as Christian Education director at the Glen Park Bible Church, Mr. Nichols?

NICHOLS: Five years now.

INTERVIEWER: During that time, would you say that you have succeeded in building a successful ministry to young teens?

NICHOLS: Yes, definitely.

INTERVIEWER: Good! What has been the key to success?

NICHOLS: I'd say that it is two youth sponsors who literally have invested their time and their lives in those kids.

INTERVIEWER: What about Sunday School—are the teens as excited about it as they are about their youth group?

NICHOLS: No way! I'm sorry to say that most of them don't like Sunday School at all.

INTERVIEWER: Why is that? What if you took those people who are working in the youth group and put them to work in the Sunday School—would the kids like it better then?

NICHOLS: I don't think so. We've preconditioned kids to think of Sunday School as a drag. After all, what do they do there? In most of the classes they've been in, all they have done is sit and listen to a teacher lecture to them for 30 minutes about something that seems to have nothing to do with the life of a teenager today. Can you see any fun in that? And how much do they learn that way? Why should we expect kids to want to be in Sunday School?

INTERVIEWER: I think you've got something there.

Sunday School can be fun!

Unfortunately, Sunday School is a "drag" for many young teens. But it doesn't have to be. It can be interesting, fun, and produce learning that changes lives. How can you make this happen in your class? There is no simple formula for successful teaching; nothing that "automatically" works. Pray and trust the Holy Spirit to enlighten and empower you, as well as to move the hearts of your students as you lead them.

In planning lessons, remember that young teens learn best when:

—they can see how Bible truth relates to their personal interests, problems, and needs.

—they are actively involved in the learning process with their teacher and the rest of the group.

—they have opportunities to respond to the truth they have discovered in the Word of God.

Put this knowledge to work for you in following a three-step guided-discovery process in your teaching:

FOCUS **1** Begin each lesson by zeroing in on a specific need or interest of young teens. Pose a question, raise an issue, or present a problem to gain attention, motivate students for the Bible study, and let them know where the lesson is heading. Then move into step 2:

DISCOVER **2** This is the longest part of the lesson, during which you and your class explore Scriptures. Using a variety of methods planned for full group participation, guide your teens in discovering truths in the Word of God, learning what they mean, and understanding the implications of those truths for their personal lives. Understanding and applying truth is closely related to step 3:

RESPOND

3

In this climax to the lesson, lead your class to ask, "How does this truth apply to us today?" And even more personally, "What is *my* response to the truth I have learned?" Then give your class opportunities and suggestions for actively expressing the decisions and commitments the Holy Spirit has led them to make.

Try it!

Let's see how these three steps might be carried out in an actual teaching situation. Suppose you are teaching a lesson based on Deuteronomy 6:1-9. Your aim: "To help each young teen understand God's plan for his parents and cooperate with them in carrying out that plan."

FOCUS

TEACHER: Parents are pretty neat people, aren't they? We may have our problems with them at times, but I think we'd all agree that we couldn't do without them. Have you ever asked yourself, "What do my parents do for me?" and really tried to give an honest answer? Let's brainstorm that question right now. I've drawn on the board three columns and labeled them: *Birth to 5 years, 6 to 12 years,* and *13 through high school.* Let's take three minutes to list as many things as you can think of that your parents do (or have done) for you during these ages in your life. I'll list them as you mention them. Then we'll talk about them.

Birth to 5 years:

JOHN: I don't remember much about when I was that young. But my parents gave me food, clothing, and a house to live in of course.

BEN: They helped us learn to walk and talk, and they played with us.

DAN: A lot of what they did was to help us learn— like giving us books and TV.

JIM: They loved us and made us feel safe. Little kids specially need those.

TEACHER: Anything else?

BILL: They took us to Sunday School with them every week.

TEACHER: Good. Anything else? *(Pauses.)* How about from *6 to 12 years?*

BILL: Well, we still needed clothes and food and a home, and they gave us all those.

DAN: They helped us get used to going to school and helped us with our homework.

JIM: They've tried to help us have good habits—like being neat and keeping our rooms clean—and also to be responsible for doing other work around the house. With me, it doesn't work so well, though!

TEACHER: These are good examples. How about your friends? Do your parents show that they are interested in the kinds of friends you have?

DAN: Oh sure. They don't want us going around with kids who take dope or do some other weird things.

JIM: Yeah, like Mark, he's really weird!

TEACHER: What about problems, which all of us have? Do your parents ever help you out with those?

JIM: Mine do, if I ask them.

BILL *(hesitantly):* Mine do when they have time.

DAN: Yeah.

JOHN: Mine *never* have time!

TEACHER Well, let's move on to *13 through high school.* You're just entering that age now, so you'll have to think ahead.

DAN: They'll still be responsible for us till we're grown up. They'll give us food, some money, a place to live, and buy our clothes. If we're sick, they'll have to pay the hospital bills.

JOHN: And they'll see that we go to school—whether we like it or not!

JIM: They'll help us decide what subjects to take in high school and maybe in college.

TEACHER: Would you say that this is the age when

your parents will counsel you about a lot of things—
such as dating and sex?

JOHN: Not me, man!

TEACHER: How about whether you should go in for
sports or music in school, whether you should have a
job—things like that?

JIM: Yeah. Sometimes they give us *too* much advice!

TEACHER: We have a good list here on the board.
Have we left out anything? *(Pause.)* I'm thinking of one
responsibility of parents that God is particularly
concerned with, which might include the things we
have listed here. What do you think it is? *(Pause.)* Bill
came close to it when he mentioned that his parents
always brought him to Sunday School. Bill—want to
say more?

BILL: Is it that God wants our parents to help us
learn about Him?

TEACHER: Yes. And that's a big job. God has told
them what to do and how to do it. Let's turn to
Deuteronomy 6:1-9 and find God's plan for our
parents. Knowing what He expects of them will help us
know how we can cooperate with them in carrying out
that plan.

DISCOVER   To appreciate the setting of this passage of Scripture, I'd like you to imagine that you are a newspaper
reporter traveling with Moses and the Israelites. It's
about 1450 B.C. You're camped on the banks of the
Jordan River, getting ready to cross into the Promised
Land. Everyone is really excited! Moses calls all the
parents together to give them some instructions from
the Lord about their families. What does Moses say?

That will be your job—to study Deuteronomy 6:1-9
and put in your own words on these sheets I am
handing out, the important things Moses told those
parents. Write as if you were making a news report.

Make up a name for your newspaper, a headline, a place, and add the date. Put your imagination into your story. You have eight minutes. *(Later, the teacher calls on two or three teens to read their articles to the class.)*

You did a good job on those. All of you brought out the three things that God wants parents to do: Know His truths, live them, and teach them to their children. Let's talk about these. As we do, I'll jot down on the chalkboard some points for us to remember.

First, Moses told parents that they were to *know God's truth,* His Word. *(Writes on board.)* What was God's Word for those Israelite parents? (It was the laws and ordinances of God that had been given to their fathers at Mt. Sinai, through Moses. Why do you think Moses reminded them about God's laws at this time?

BILL: Weren't these different people now?

TEACHER: Right. The new generation probably had forgotten most of them, so as they gathered at the banks of the Jordan River, looking forward to the conquest of the Promised Land, Moses repeated the Law to them.

What was it that Moses really emphasized about God's commands? *(Waits for teens to think and respond.)*

JIM: The people were supposed to obey them.

TEACHER: Yes! If a person is to obey an order from a person in authority, he must first of all know what the order is. Isn't this true in our relationship with God? *(Pauses.)* The first step is to know what God has told us—what He wants His children to be and do.

Moses explained to the Israelite parents God's reasons for giving His people commandments and laws. What were God's reasons? *(Waits for teens to review verses.)*

BILL *(reads from v. 2):* It says, "So that you and

your son and your grandson might fear the Lord your God," and "that it may be well with you and that you may multiply greatly."

TEACHER: Yes. Do you see where God wanted His laws to lead the people? *(Pauses.)* Into a relationship of reverence and trust with Him that would result in their happiness and prosperity.

What would be the result of the Jewish parents' following God's commands? *(Pauses while teens think.)*

DAN: Verses 2 and 3 say that they would have long, happy years in Canaan and have many children.

BILL: Also, they would be a great nation, in a land flowing with milk and honey.

TEACHER: Today we have much more of God's Word than those Jewish parents had. Does God bless parents today who live by His truth and lead their families according to the teachings in His Word? We may be sure God will bless them. Let's read two of His promises to do this. *(The class reads together Psalms 19:11 and 128:1-2.)*

Now let's talk about the second thing God requires of parents: to live His truth *(writes on board)*. In your study guide there are some questions to help you. Bill, start us off in discussing the first one now: "What did Moses mean by parents having God's words in their hearts?"

BILL: Well, I'm not sure. . . . He couldn't have meant their real hearts. . . . That wouldn't make sense.

TEACHER: No. . . . Anyone else want to add anything? What does the word *heart* mean here?

JOHN: Is it . . . the inside of a person?

DAN: Would it be what a person thinks and wants . . . maybe the reasons for doing what he does?

TEACHER: I think we're all getting the same idea. This passage is teaching that God's Word is to so fill parents' lives that every part of them—even the very deepest—is affected by it. This has a *godly* effect on their children. *(Pauses.)*

What are some of the effects on kids when their parents live in a way that contradicts what they teach?

BILL: The kids won't listen to a thing they tell them . . . They usually do just the opposite.

TEACHER: Yes. . . . Who can put into one statement what God wants parents to do about living His truth? Bill?

BILL: How about *(pauses)*, "God wants parents to be good examples of Christ to their children."

TEACHER: Fine! *(Writes on board.)*

Now let's go to the third responsibility God gives to parents. What is it? . . . John, will you remind us?

JOHN: Is it in verse 7? It says, to teach God's words to their children . . . when they "sit . . . work . . . lie down . . . rise up."

TEACHER *(writing on board):* What do you think this means? What is *teaching* God's Word? How is it different from or similar to *talking about* God's Word?

JIM: Is teaching what Sunday School teachers do and talking what parents do?

TEACHER: Maybe that's the way it seems. But according to this passage, whose responsibility is it to teach in a regular systematic way what God's Word says? *(Pauses.)*

Why is it so important to learn from our parents what the Bible actually says?

BILL: What my parents always say is, so that I will have something to guide me when I have to make decisions.

TEACHER: Good, Bill. We need to have a store of God's truth to draw on, don't we? *(Pauses.)*

How can parents teach their children? Any ideas?

JIM: Would they have to have a certain day for it?

And a certain time? . . . Like Sunday School?

TEACHER: What do you think? Do any of your parents do it like that? *(Pauses for responses.)*

JOHN: Nope, never!

JIM: Sometimes on Sunday afternoons we go over the lessons we've had in Sunday School. And once our family studied a short book of the Bible together . . . I think it was James.

TEACHER: Probably *talking about* God's truth is more common in our homes. This is an informal way parents guide us in responding to God. In what ways have your parents shared God's truth with you during some of your daily activities?

JIM: Ever since my sister and I were little kids, either my mom or dad has talked with us a few minutes at night, in our rooms. We usually get started just talking about what has happened during school.

TEACHER: Great, Jim! *(Pauses.)* Anyone else?

BILL: Sometimes my dad talks to me when we're at ball games. I like it better that way . . . he doesn't preach at me, just talks.

TEACHER: That's the best way, isn't it, Dan? *(To the class):* Do you think this passage of Scripture means that parents are to quote Scriptures to their kids all the time?

JIM: No—at least I hope not.

BILL: I think it means what Dan said . . . that our parents should talk with us about God's Word wherever it fits into what we're doing.

TEACHER: Anyone else have another opinion? *(Pauses.)* I can remember when I was a teenager. . . . I was sitting with my dad on the steps of our vacation cabin one night. Something had been bothering me for a long time—and all of a sudden I just opened up and spilled everything. Dad was really surprised that I had the problem. But he had faced one almost like it, and he showed me in his Bible the words the Lord had used to help him find a solution. We read the Bible and prayed, and through that experience the Lord kept me from committing a terrible sin. You can be sure I've thanked the Lord for a dad who gave me the right kind of counsel just when I needed it.

DAN: Yeah, but my dad's not like that. He's never home, and when he is, he's always so busy!

TEACHER: I understand your situation, Dan. All of us have problems of one kind or another in our homes. Have you thought about what you might do to help your dad when he is home? Maybe we can talk about it.

RESPOND   In fact, how can we all help our parents carry out God's plan for passing on His truth to us? *(Waits for responses.)*

Notice the chart in your study guides. It suggests 15 different actions that you might carry out in your home. For instance, one is, "Pray for my mom and dad, that God will give them wisdom in teaching me." I've made a large copy of this chart for the overhead projector, in case you don't have your books here. *(Shows transparency.)* Take three minutes to read the list and check those actions which you feel apply to your situation, and which you see as your responsibilities. We'll talk about any that you wish to. Then we'll pray, asking the Lord to give us the courage and strength to follow through on our good intentions. Let's each pray a sentence prayer for the person on his left, asking God to help him in his home this week.

Make it yours

You'll want to scan the lesson again, as you think about these questions:
1. What words describe this teacher's way of teaching?

    telling   sharing   preaching   leading
        reading   conversing   guiding
2. List all the ways the teacher involved the students.

3. Do you think the teacher created a good atmosphere for learning in his class? In what way or ways?
4. What visuals and equipment did the teacher use?
5. What kinds of questions did the teacher use? For what purposes?
6. In what ways did the teacher share with his class his experience of the truths he was teaching?
7. Did he keep the class on the subject? How?
8. What use did he make of the student's study guide?
9. What did the teacher do to help create a sense of oneness and caring among the members of his class?
10. What is *guided discovery learning?*

Knowing your goals
4

Nothing could be more true in teaching junior highs. It is important to set specific, measurable goals and periodically evaluate whether you are reaching them.

WHAT ARE YOUR GOALS?

What do you want to accomplish as a Christian teacher of young teens? Your goals will probably fall into these broad areas of Christian education:

1. Leading students into a basic knowledge of biblical facts and concepts.
2. Helping affect changes in students' attitudes.
3. Communicating the Christian faith and values.

What you want to do in these areas will give you direction for your weekly sessions and unit studies.

Leading students into a basic knowledge of biblical facts and concepts

Basic to all Christian education is the faithful teaching of biblical information. Some teachers neglect this part of their ministry to young teens, concentrating only on building relationships with their students. That is important, but it is not enough by itself. Students

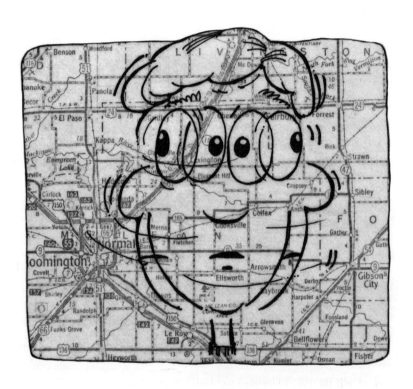

IF YOU DON'T KNOW WHERE YOU'RE GOING, YOU'RE CERTAIN TO END UP SOMEWHERE ELSE.

must have regular, comprehensive Bible study if they are to know Christ, grow, and develop. (A knowledge of the Bible is indispensable for Sunday School teachers as well.)

At the same time, biblical information taught without consideration for the needs, interests, and abilities of young teens is usually uninteresting and meaningless to them.

Do you have an overall plan for teaching Bible doctrines to your class? If you teach for one year, how much will they have learned? After young teens have been in your department (two or three years, depending on your grading system), how much Bible knowledge will they have acquired? Has your Christian Education committee or departmental leader guided you in setting up these knowledge goals for your students?

Publishers of the Sunday School curriculum you use have carefully developed units of study that fit young teens' needs and developmental abilities, and provide a solid foundation of Bible truth. If you study that plan, and the goals of each unit of study, you will have an overall view of the parts of the Bible your teens will cover.

What you teach your young teens should build on what they have been taught in the junior department. Your students should be increasing in their knowledge of basic doctrines such as these:

God

God exists in three Persons—Father, Son, and Holy Spirit.

God created all things and governs all things.

God is personally concerned about individuals.

God justifies by His grace all who receive His Son by faith.

God desires that we commune with Him through prayer, and answers His children when they call on Him.

We are to love God with all our heart, soul, mind, and strength.

Young teens should have a growing realization that fellowship with God increases a believer's recognition of God's working in his life. They should have a deeper understanding of justification, and how God's Law expressed in the Ten Commandments is comprehended and deepened in Christ's "Great Commandment." The fact that they are accountable to God for their actions is also essential for them to learn.

Jesus Christ

Jesus Christ is the Son of God, equal and co-eternal with God the Father. He also is truly Man, who, during his life on earth, was tempted in all ways as we are but lived without sinning.

Young teens should be growing in an understanding of what salvation is and how to share this knowledge with others. All they have assimilated about the Lord Jesus—that He is Shepherd, Friend, Redeemer, and coming King—should increase their appreciation for the complete provision which a believer has in Christ, for past sins, present living, and life after death.

Holy Spirit

Young teens should know that the Holy Spirit shares the nature and attributes of God the Father and God the Son. He works in unbelievers to convict them of sin, and lives in believers to sanctify and empower them to live for God in this world.

The Bible

Young teens should see the Bible as God's inspired, infallible revelation of Himself to people, and the chief means by which the Holy Spirit convicts of sin, and equips believers for spiritual living.

Young teens should learn how the Old and New Testaments fit together, and the overall messages of each.

In their studies, young teens need to become familiar with the biblical accounts of the main events in the life of Jesus, on new levels of their understanding. They should also understand the relationship of prophecy to its fulfillment in Jesus Christ.

The church

An important part of teens' learning is the teaching that the church is the body of Christ, made up of all true believers in Him. Each believer has at least one spiritual gift to be used in building up the body. Every believer should actively confess his faith in Christ and become a part of a local body of believers to minister and be ministered to, and become a witness for the Lord in his community.

Helping to affect changes in students' attitudes

As young teens grow, they should increasingly recognize that the Christian life is an active life of obedience to God, fellowship with

Him, and service to others. God has a life-purpose for each believer, and will guide us each day as we live in fellowship with Him. God wants His children to pray, study His Word, show the fruit of the Spirit, and love and serve others.

In your classroom, you can use the Word of God, the influence of the group, and various learning experiences to mold the attitudes of your students toward God, His people, and non-Christians.

Evaluating how much factual information your teens are gaining can be simply done through periodic end-of-lesson and unit reviews, tests, and checks. But evaluating progress in the area of attitude changes and the following area is more difficult.

Communicating the Christian faith and values

What we value determines our morality—our right and wrong behavior. The values of Christians are to be based on the teachings of Scripture. For instance, Christians should love people and regard them as having very high value, because Jesus Christ loves them and gave up His life for their salvation (John 3:16-17). Throughout the Bible, in both Old and New Testaments, and especially in the life of

Jesus, we find virtues we should value, and illustrations of them: kindness, justice, honesty, compassion, mercy, regard for others' property, concern for the poor, and many more.

In recent years, there has been a new emphasis on moral education in public schools. No doubt this has resulted from concern over the moral crises we are experiencing in our nation. According to a report by the Princeton Religion Research Center, "Violence, crime, and lawlessness is on the increase. One person in four nationwide has been mugged, robbed, assaulted, or had his home broken into at least once during the 12-month period tested.

"Alcohol abuse and drug dependency are reaching epidemic proportions.

"Discipline is named by parents as the top problem facing the schools in their communities. Hundreds of teachers are physically attacked each month by their students and thousands of school children are physically abused. A recent Gallup Youth Survey indicated that as many as one teenager in five is fearful of bodily injury during school hours.

"Cheating in schools and colleges is widespread. By their own admission, most of America's teenagers—six in ten—have cheated on a school exam."*

One way moral education is carried out in schools is through *values clarification* activities. In this process, teachers present situations to the class that will help students clarify what is important to them. Students discuss the facts, explore reasoning, and try to predict consequences of various actions.

According to Bonnidell Clouse, professor of educational psychology at Indiana State University in Terre Haute, "Seven criteria must be met for a child to choose a value. He must: (1) be able to choose freely, without the restriction of authoritarian rules; (2) consider alternatives; (3) choose only after thoughtfully considering the consequences of each alternative; (4) be happy with his choice; (5) affirm the choice publicly; (6) act upon it; and (7) incorporate the behavior into his life pattern. Areas such as money, friendship, love,

---

Religion in America 1979-1980. Introduction.

leisure, politics, maturity, religion, and morals are fertile ground for values clarification. The teacher needs to provide the opportunity for a child to express his ideas, must accept these expressions nonjudgmentally, and should encourage the student to consider the ideas of others."*

Values clarification recognizes that values, to be real and lasting, must come from inside a person. They can't be imposed on him by teachers, friends, or even his parents. However, Christians can't agree with the basic assumption of the values clarification approach, which is that there are no absolute values. Christians believe that the values revealed in the Bible are absolute. If a person's feelings, desires, or reasonings conflict with what the Bible teaches, he is to do what God says.

The values clarification approach is different from that of *moral judgment,* another approach to moral education. This approach, developed by Jean Piaget and Lawrence Kohlberg, holds that certain values *are* more desirable than others. Kohlberg taught that persons advance through six stages of moral development, and also that true morality comes from within. But the *moral judgment* approach separates moral development from a religious base.

In the *moral judgment* approach, moral dilemmas are presented and each student must decide how he would solve them and why. Teachers are not to say who is right and who is wrong. It is desirable for a student to move from one stage of moral reasoning to another, but he must move at his own pace, without being judged or pressured. Sometimes the reasoning of his classmates can help him move to a higher level of reasoning.

Kohlberg's theories contain good psychological insights. But believers need to add biblical insights to them to affect moral education that is truly Christian.

Will your students have Christian values?

If you carefully and prayerfully prepare and teach your lessons each week, can you be sure your students will make Christian values their

---

*"Reading, Writing, And . . . Right from Wrong?" *Christianity Today,* December 30, 1977.

own? No, unfortunately. Recent studies indicate that, in general, today's Christian young people are not relating Christianity to their personal lives and are developing value systems quite different from those of their Christian parents and teachers.

Why is this? In many cases, it is not because they have not been exposed to the clear teachings of God's Word. Contrarily, most of them have had years of teaching in Sunday School and church. Two reasons why many young people do not adapt the values of their Christian parents and teachers are: (1) they do not see those values being modeled, and (2) they have not been given the opportunity to honestly think through what they believe for themselves. What this means is, they have simply been indoctrinated with the truth and not made it a part of their own value systems.

As with faith, values are most easily caught than taught. In your weekly contacts with your students, what are you showing them about your *real* values, not what you *say* are your values?

In each weekly session, what do you do to help your young people work through matters that are important to determining values? Young adolescents are just beginning a long process of sorting out what is important to them. They need to express their doubts and challenge concepts they have easily accepted up to this time. They need many opportunities to make choices between competing value systems they see displayed in adults and the world around them. Through these struggles they come to know what they truly believe and value.

Offer your young teens many different learning experiences, both structured and unstructured, in which they go through a decision-making process. As you guide them, frequently ask, "Why?" This will help them explore their feelings and reasonings more deeply, arriving at their own choices. They will do this best in a climate of openness and acceptance, where they don't have to fear being criticized for their feelings or pressured into "accepting" values they have not investigated.

In every lesson you prepare, ask the Holy Spirit to help you relate the truth to the needs of your students. Go beyond merely exposing them to information. Help them see what it has to do with their everyday lives. Then, as Dr. Lois LeBar points out in her book, *Education That Is Christian,* they will become interested in the truth, and through the working of the Spirit in their hearts, want to do something about the truth, till finally they are controlled by the truth, making it the basis for the actions of their entire lives. And the following prayer will be true of them: "Thy Word have I hid [made a working principle] in my heart, that I might not sin against Thee" (Ps. 119:11).

Make it yours

1. What do you use as an evaluation tool to determine whether your students are learning desired Bible facts and concepts? If you do not have one, determine how you will evaluate your teaching in this basic area.
2. How should Bible information be taught, to help young teens make it a part of their daily lives?
3. What is the difference between the *values clarification* and the *moral judgment* approaches to moral education?
4. Think of your last teaching session. What kind of learning climate characterized your classroom? What did you do to help teens think through what they really believe and make biblical principles the bases of their value systems?
5. What are you learning about your own value system as you struggle with current issues and endeavor to relate Christianity to them?

Preparing yourself and the lesson
5

At 7:20 on Saturday night George remembered that he had not yet studied his Sunday School lesson. He found his *teacher's manual* and looked at the theme. It was love—showing people that we really care about them. "This is a good one," he said to himself. "The kids really need this." He flipped over a few pages. The lesson was based on a familiar passage of Scripture—1 Corinthians 13. He had read that chapter dozens of times and could talk on it for an hour. He wouldn't have to study it again. And the lesson outline was simple enough. He'd just cut it out of his book, stick it in his Bible, and refer to it in class. George read the lesson through once and closed his manual.

Many teachers are like George, waiting till Saturday night to prepare their lessons and depending a little on the helps in their *teachers' manuals* to "bail them out." As a result, they fail to achieve the satisfying and lasting results they may genuinely want to achieve.

Let's go back to George and see how things went in his classroom the following Sunday:

George had covered the first two points in his lesson outline without any interruptions. *I'm doing pretty well,* he thought. But it was too good to be true. Bob, an especially bright and thoughtful kid, stopped him with a question. George felt impatient. He hadn't expected this. If he didn't hurry, he would never get through all his material. He gave Bob a quick answer and went on. But the boy still didn't understand and stopped his teacher again. This time George snapped at him.

It was easy to see that Bob was embarrassed. He obviously felt stupid for having asked his question and didn't say another word. Everyone else in class grew quiet too. But George didn't notice the quietness.

George talked 20 minutes more. At last he had covered all the material under the last point in his outline. It was time to make an application. He told his class they should think about whether they really show love to other people. Then he asked them to bow their heads and confess to the Lord their sin of failing to be loving and kind. He asked someone to pray aloud but no one did, so George prayed. After class, he said to himself, "I wish every lesson were this easy." But still he had a nagging sense that something was wrong— that he hadn't really done his job well.

George's failure to communicate in class began with his failure to prepare adequately at home. And his failure to take the time for adequate preparation stemmed from his failure to understand what teaching is.

Your aim each week should be to communicate to your teens, in the power of the Holy Spirit, one main concept from God's Word and encourage them to respond positively to that truth. But you can't do this unless you have meditated on that truth and allowed it to affect your own thinking and living as a follower of Jesus.

Preparing yourself

It is important that you begin your lesson preparation early in the week. Why? Because not only do you need time to prepare material, but you need time to prepare *yourself*.

Shortness of time for lesson preparation may be a problem you will always have to hassle with. Family and work responsibilities may not let you put your class at the top of your priorities list. By making a real effort, however, and carefully reshuffling some things in your schedule, you can find more time for thorough preparation than you think you have.

Early in the week, Monday if possible, begin your lesson preparation with prayer. Ask the Holy Spirit to give you a quiet mind and heart, enabling you to concentrate on His Word, and to make the Word clear, helping you understand what it says. Pray that as He prepares you this week, He will work in a similar way in the daily lives of your students.

Read the passage of Scripture that the lesson is based on. Try not to think of your class at this time or how you will present the material. Consider first what is taught in the passage and then what God says to you through it. Ask yourself questions, and write down the answers. "Who are the main people in this passage (if any)? What are they doing? Where is the action taking place? What can I learn from their experiences? What can I learn about God and His will for me from this passage? What prompted the writing of these words? What command, promise, advice, warning, or instruction do they hold for me?"

Carefully determine the main idea or teaching in the passage. (Is it the love of God for sinners? Christ's death and resurrection? The tie that binds believers? The Christian's responsibility in this world? The fact that people are made in God's image?) Once you have discovered the outstanding truth, write it down. Do you understand it, or does it confuse you? Do you believe it? Have you experienced it? Is it something you never realized before? Pray, asking the Holy Spirit to make that lesson truth a reality in your daily life throughout the coming week.

For the next few days, look for the Spirit's working out of that truth through the people and circumstances surrounding you. Wherever you are, whatever you are doing, ask the divine indwelling Teacher to speak to you about what you read and use experiences from your life to fill in the blanks in your understanding, answer your questions, and confirm and illustrate the truthfulness of His Word. On the same sheet where you recorded your first reactions, write down what you observe, what your thoughts and feelings tell you about the subject of the lesson. Keep a mini-"spiritual diary" as you daily follow the Holy Spirit through the lesson of your own experience.

Preparing the lesson

When you continue your preparation later in the week, read the lesson in your *teacher's manual* thoroughly. See how it fits in with the rest of the lessons in the unit by reviewing each week's aims. Does this week's lesson aim express what God has taught you this week? Do you want your teens to experience this truth, as you have? Write down, in a simple sentence, the one thing that you want your kids to begin to know, feel, and do, as a result of their studying this part of God's Word together on Sunday.

Carefully read the lesson in the *student's study guide,* trying to see it from the teens' point of view. Then, with your aim in mind, adapt the lesson in your *teacher's manual* to fit your class and the amount of time you will have for teaching. Listen to the *Young Teen Teacher Cassette,* for additional Bible background and teaching ideas. Also prepare the visual correlated with your curriculum in the *Teaching Aid Packet,* or create your own.

Plan ways to involve your teens in the learning process, choosing methods that will lead them to ask some of the same questions about the Scripture passage that you asked in your personal study during the week. Prepare to discuss those questions. Think of individual students and the problems and needs in their lives which relate to the lesson theme. Plan how you will apply specific parts of the lesson to those needs. Then pray that the Holy Spirit will minister to hearts as you faithfully present His Word and relate in a warm, caring way to your kids.

Finally, on a 4" x 6" card, transfer the lesson aim, methods, and activities you will use for each part of the lesson—*Focus, Discover, Respond.* (At the end of this chapter there is a sample card for the lesson in chapter 3.) When you go to Sunday School, take with you this card, your Bible, your *student's manual,* and your prepared classroom visuals.

If you always make it your aim to start lesson preparation early in the week, Saturday night will find you relaxed and confident. You will have time to review your lesson plan and pray again for God to work through you as you teach your class the next day. He promises to bless such faithfulness!

God's family plan
(Deut. 6:1-9)

AIM: To help each young teen understand God's plan for his parents and cooperate with them in carrying out that plan.

FOCUS (5 minutes)*	Put three columns on the chalkboard and label them *birth to 5 years, 6 to 12 years,* and *13 through high school.* Teens brainstorm about what parents do for them during these ages, and list ideas in the proper columns.
DISCOVER (20-25 minutes)	(1) Teens write a news report based on Deuteronomy 6:1-9 to discover the instructions God told Moses to tell parents. (2) A few teens read their articles aloud. (3) List main points on the chalkboard: Know God's truth Live God's truth Teach God's truth (4) Guide understanding through questions. Discuss questions in the student's guide: "What did Moses mean by parents having God's words in their hearts?" and "What are usually the effects on children when their parents live in a way that contradicts what they teach?" (5) Share a personal experience as an illustration of today's truth.
RESPOND (5-10 minutes)	(1) Teens check on a chart the actions they want to carry out at home this week (chart is in *study guide* and on the overhead transparency). (2) Each teen prays for the person on his left, that God will help him in his home this week.

* Time spent on each step will vary from lesson to lesson.

Make it yours

1. Why is it wise to begin your lesson preparation early in the week?
2. What spiritual insights have you gained in your lesson preparation? What are some ways to help your teens make similar discoveries?
3. Analyze how you usually prepare your lesson, and how much time you spend. What will you do to change or improve some habits? What adjustments do you need to make in your schedule of time and activities to insure these improvements?
4. Begin, or continue to prepare, Sunday's lesson today.

Exploring
ways to teach
6

The boys' eighth-grade teacher was absorbed in his lecture. But his students were lost in their own thoughts:

"What a drag! He talks all the time."

"My teacher doesn't even know I'm alive."

"The kids in this class sure are unfriendly."

"Why can't we talk about something I'm interested in?"

"I already *know* the problem. But what's the solution?"

"I'd like to ask him, but I'm afraid he'd be too shocked."

"Doesn't God care about what's happening in the world today? Can't we talk about it?"

A teacher who does all the talking in his classroom is a teacher who soon finds himself asking, "What went wrong?" But a teacher who motivates his group to join in the teaching-learning process is appealing to the teens' need to be involved in discovering truths for themselves. He or she is tapping the rich potential young people have of learning from each other and is insuring that they won't become bored in his class.

In meeting the needs of people He encountered, Jesus the Master Teacher used a variety of methods: parables, questions, lecture-sermons, experience, object lessons, problem-solving, and illustrations. To do your best at the teaching task to which He has called you, follow His example. Methods in themselves do not change lives; only the Holy Spirit can do this. But He may choose to work through carefully planned teaching techniques to carry out His divine plans, just as He chooses to move the hearts of your young people and mold their personalities through the example of your dedicated life.

What methods should I use?

There is no one best way to teach. Two teachers can teach the same lesson using different methods and achieve the same results. In one lesson you will probably use two or more methods. Varying them from week to week will keep your lessons fresh.

Begin by making your teaching conversational, rather than just telling your class what the Scriptures say. Use an informal *question and answer* approach, whether in studying a Scripture passage, reviewing important facts, or talking about practical problems. Encourage your teens to think for themselves and share insights with each other. Using key questions, draw out important ideas that will help the lesson move toward its planned conclusion. Word your questions carefully and write them out in your notes.

Your *student's Bible study guide* offers a wealth of opportunities for varying your classtime activities. It presents assignments for teens to do, illustrations to refer to, checklists to complete, questions to discuss, problems to solve, and projects to make.

Discussion. Most 12- to 14-year-olds are masters of small talk. Most of them are also capable of thinking seriously about important problems of life. You might be amazed if you could see your young teens enthusiastically taking part in discussions in school.

Discussion is more than question-and-answer. A question for discussion must involve probing and give students opportunities to express their views. It is not one that can be answered with a yes or no or a simple statement of fact, such as: "How many wives did Solomon have?"; "Was Jesus ever baptized?"; or "What did Jesus do to pay for our sins?" Neither should a discussion question be so vague that students don't know how to respond ("How is death the wages of sin?"); nor so broad that teens answer in unsatisfactory generalities. ("How can we show we are Christians?") A better question, one that would encourage dialogue, would be, "How can we show we are Christians when there is a death in the family of a friend?"

To touch off interest, you might present an understandable and interesting *problem to solve*. For example: "If the Lord Jesus were here today, what attitudes or practices would He condemn in your school?" If the kids mention cheating, you might follow up with: "Why is cheating contrary to the kind of life Christ wants you to live? Is helping someone with his homework cheating? When might it become cheating? What can you do to discourage cheating in your school?"

You may wish to begin a discussion by telling an open-end story like the one used by a teacher in Niles, Iowa:

"Calvary Church had one of the best missionary conventions they have ever had. At the close of it, four young people said they believed God had called them to be witnesses for Him in foreign lands.

"Jim, who was already expecting to be a missionary, signed a faith-promise card. This means that Jim will trust the Lord to provide him with an amount of money which he will give to the church within a year, for a special missionary project they are supporting. Jim's promise is for $15.

"Six months have gone by, and as yet Jim does not have the money. No one knows about his faith-promise. But he is thinking about telling his parents. Why do you think he wants to? Should he? What should he do? Why?"

An open-end story, like this one is mind-stretching and stimulating to young people. But all discussions do not have to center on problem-solving. You may ask a question about a Bible person or situation and assign students to find information in the Word. Each one may give an opinion, based on what he has read. Write their answers on the board and discuss each in turn.

Young teens are good at getting off the track, so you will have to be alert for unrelated comments and steer the discussion back to the subject without cutting anyone off. ("You've brought up a good point that I'd like to discuss fully another time, Jim. The question we'd like to focus on right now is . . .")

Try to draw into your discussions the more reserved students as well as the naturally talkative ones. Avoid always calling on the first person who wishes to contribute; give the guy or gal who doesn't often volunteer a chance to speak. Prompt those teens to respond who usually just sit and listen, by using questions such as, "Bill, how do you feel about that?" or "Louise, how would you handle this kind of problem?"

To hold a good discussion, work on cultivating an open learning climate in your classroom. Does every student feel accepted by the other members of the group? Does each teen feel free to express himself frankly, without fear of being laughed at or criticized? Good discussions involve good thinking, and good thinking results when students are not afraid to honestly say what they feel.

Brainstorming may precede a discussion. This involves listing on the board or large sheet of paper as many ideas as teens can supply on a given subject or problem, without any comments or criticisms being given. After all the ideas are compiled, teens may go back and consider each idea on the list, evaluating it fully.

Role playing. A good way to help teens identify with persons in a Bible narrative or a real-life situation is to have them spontaneously act out a brief scene. This is not acting or dramatics, but a means of helping teens understand or learn how others feel in situations unfamiliar to them. For instance, what's it like to be a pastor, a mother, or an elderly person who lives alone?

In an Illinois Sunday School, role playing was carried on in a combined girls' and boys' class. As an introduction to a lesson on the prodigal son, two students were asked to put themselves in the place of a modern runaway teenage son who is being interviewed by a reporter. To prepare them for this role, the teacher asked them to sit in their chairs in a manner they thought the young rebel would sit, and to change their clothing in any way they would like to fit their role. Both students casually draped themselves in their seats; the boy opened his jacket and unbuttoned part of his shirt; the girl kicked off her shoes. Then the interview began:

"When did you first think about running away from home?"

"Oh . . . ever since I was a little kid I've thought about it, I guess."

"Would you tell us why?"

"I always felt like I was in the way. There were so many kids at home, nobody ever had time for me."

"And now that you're growing up . . ."

"It's not any different. My parents don't even know I'm around, most of the time."

And so the interview went, the interviewer asking questions that would help the teens identify with the runaway whose role they were playing. The questions also prepared the entire class for the Bible study by helping them feel what rebelliousness is and understand some causes behind it.

In the classroom where the role playing was done, an excellent example of *team-teaching* was carried out. Husband and wife worked together in leading various parts of the lesson: she, the introductory role play; he, the main Bible study. Each commented freely throughout the discussion.

Lecture summary. Sometimes it helps to present certain facts or summarize part of a lesson. For instance, you may want to give your teens some additional historical background about a biblical city or custom that they can't find in their Bibles. When you do the talking, be carefully prepared and speak enthusiastically, always keeping eye contact with your group. Naturally this means that you should not read lengthy excerpts from a book. Nothing will cause you to lose your teens' attention more quickly than this!

One good way to hold attention during a lecture, as well as improve your teens' understanding and retention of what you tell them, is to write key words on the chalkboard as you speak or to illustrate your talk with simple drawings on the chalkboard. You may do the drawings beforehand on a flip chart. By turning the pages as you cover points in your lecture, you will keep your teens' interest, for they'll be anticipating what is next.

Another way to add spark to a lecture is to plan it well enough ahead of time so you can invite your class to bring in objects, pictures, or other visuals to illustrate the topic and add to the information you will give. Then, at the appropriate times, you can invite students to share what they have brought.

Lecturing is effective if it is brief, illustrated, presented on the teens' level of interest and understanding, and is not used too often. But most teachers overdo this method.

A *Scripture search* is a good way to lead teens to find out what the Bible says about a topic or doctrine. Write out various references on slips of paper, pass these out to students, and have them look up the references. Then call on each teen to tell in his own words what the verse says. In assigning verses, always have them written out on paper or on the board. Otherwise, some teens will forget and you will have to repeat what you've told them. This means a loss of valuable time.

Research reports. During the week, call a capable and dependable student and ask him to prepare a report on a given topic. Offer reference books for him to use, or suggest where he might locate some, as in your church or public library. Also be ready to spend some time with him to give him any help he needs. The information you want him to present may be in your *teacher's manual.* In this case, type it out for him or let him borrow your manual.

Buzz groups. Divide your class into two or more small groups for discussion or special Bible study. Make your assignments specific; write them on the board before class or type them on cards and hand them to the groups. Appoint a recorder in each group who will, after the class reassembles, report on his group's findings or conclusions.

Listening teams. Assign groups to watch for various emphases or answers to questions as given by a speaker, film, or "voice" on a tape recording. Hold a discussion later.

Circle conversation. Each teen, beginning with one person and continuing around the group, airs his opinion or answer to a question.

Creative writing. Encourage teens to express truths they have experienced by writing poems, cinquains, limericks, short stories, or sayings. Don't sell your teens short. They think seriously about God, the Christian life, and the way the world is.

Sight and sound in your teaching

Implementing methods with visuals and audiovisuals can help you communicate beyond the abstractions of verbal language, providing added meaning and depth for your students and helping make learning exciting. Some aids you will want to use often are the *Young Teen Teacher Cassette* and the *Teaching Aid Packet*, films, filmstrips with records, the overhead projector, and cassette recorder.

Young teens of this generation are especially geared to sound. Almost all of them have TVs and transistor radios, and many have stereos and recorders of their own. Tapes and records are excellent tools to arouse attention, spark a discussion, and wrap up a lesson. In one class, for example, teens listened to a cassette tape of a mother describing the circumstances of her daughter's death. Then the class discussed what death means to a Christian, and why the mother was able to remain peaceful and hopeful throughout the experience of sorrow.

Here are some ideas for using tapes:

1. Have teens tape interviews and play them in class. For instance, they might ask people, "What do you think of Jesus Christ?" or "What is heaven like?" The class can listen and discuss responses given in the light of Scripture.

2. Record how-to information from your pastor or an outstanding youth leader. He might share with teens how to read their Bibles or have devotions, or how to get along with their parents. Keep the segments brief and play them as they fit into your prepared lesson.

3. Record parts of youth meetings or workshops and play them in class.

4. Record songs, commercials, parts of news broadcasts and panel discussions that you hear on radio or TV and use them to initiate discussion or illustrate points.

5. Let your teens make the recordings as well as listen to them. They may dramatize a Bible passage, write a script, and record it, complete with sound effects. They may also make their own slides and sound track.

6. Take your cassette on a field trip to record on-the-spot reactions and play them later in class.

An overhead projector is also a versatile and practical aid, especially for use in a large classroom or general assembly area. With this aid you can face your class while you write or draw on a transparency with a grease pencil or fiber-tip pen and project a large image on the wall. You can prepare outlines, diagrams, cartoons, charts, or maps in vivid colors ahead of time, and fill them in, trace on them, or use them in any number of ways while you are projecting them. Buy ready-made transparencies or make your own on acetate film, or prepare them from paper masters and run them through a thermal copy machine.

Using variety in your teaching methods will keep your kids coming to class and enjoying the learning experiences they have there. Aim to be a learning, creative teacher—always alert to new and better ways of teaching your teens!

Make it yours

1. What methods do you use over and over again? Are they the best ways to teach, or are you in a rut?
2. List 10 new methods you have not tried, but which you think could be effective in your class.
3. Look at next week's lesson. Plan how to use at least two new methods for variety and interest.
4. How might you use sight and sound in next week's lesson?
5. Visit your church's audiovisual library to see what materials and equipment are available for you to use.

Using the total hour to teach
7

"The opening assembly in our young teen department is a big waste of time, as far as I am concerned. What we do has no plan to it. We sing about six different songs; there are usually a lot of announcements about young people's meetings and parties; and the leader talks to the kids about things that have nothing at all to do with the lesson."

This is how one teacher described the opening assembly in her young teen department. Now listen to her departmental leader's view of the assembly:

"As I see it, the purpose of the assembly is to help the kids get to know each other better and have a time of fellowship. That's why I have all of them sitting in a circle. After all, this is the only time during the week when all of them are together. I'm not really concerned about how much time we take, or what we talk about, if everyone is involved."

These greatly differing viewpoints suggest some questions that are important to your own teaching task: What is the purpose of the opening assembly in your young teen department? Why is it important for your leader and the teachers in your department to agree on what will be done in the assembly? How can your leader use his part of the Sunday School hour to reinforce the teaching-learning process that goes on in your class?

What makes a good assembly?

Notice students in the young teen assembly of another Sunday School: They sing as if they really enjoy it; they read from their Bibles enthusiastically, and respond with interest to their leader's comments.

Observe a second group and you see young people walking into the room minutes after starting time. Some look bored; others laugh and talk openly with others.

What makes the difference between these two kinds of assemblies? Several factors determine whether an assembly is meaningful and worthwhile, or just a waste of time for both students and teachers.

Preplanning. The departmental leader should spend enough time planning and preparing at home to know exactly what he will do and how much time it will take. When he arrives (early) in the department, he makes sure songbooks are on chairs, and available for a pianist, guitarist, or other music leader. If displays are to be arranged, prayer requests to be written on the chalkboard, visual aids to be set up, and so forth, he takes care of all these ahead of time. Ready when the teens arrive, the leader is free to concentrate on them, talking with them about their weekday activities or helping them with class or department projects.

An understanding of what the assembly is for. The opening assembly, or *Group time,* should provide for planned fellowship and inspiration, and be meaningfully related to the lesson that follows. *Group time* is usually only a 10-15 minute part of the Sunday School hour, leaving most of the time for Bible instruction in class. Think of the total hour like this:

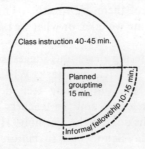

An informal fellowship time may take place for 10-15 minutes, from the arrival of the first student till the start of *Group time.* During this unstructured time, teens may talk with teachers and each other, review memory verses, make bulletin board displays, even sing favorite Christian songs.

Because *Group time* is closely related to the lesson aim of the day, the departmental leader needs to read carefully the lesson in the *Young teen teacher's manual,* as well as the suggestions for his own participation.

Opportunities for teens to participate. If teens are merely observers in *Group time,* they will soon turn off to what's happening. They are more capable than many adults think, and can plan meaningful activities related to the lesson. Those who participate need to plan their parts during the week or beforehand on Sunday. The more often they take part, the more they improve. Teens may sing, play instruments, read Scripture or dialogues, act in skits, present visuals, and more. But the departmental leader should supervise and follow up on all assignments he makes, for young teens often forget to follow through on projects they began enthusiastically.

How can you help your department leader?

Your department leader extends and reinforces your Bible-teaching ministry if he correlates the assembly with the aim of your lesson. Now, how can you best cooperate with your leader in strengthening your joint ministry to teens?

- Be at Sunday School every week, always on time, and before your students arrive.
- During the assembly time, sit with your class and participate with them.
- In teaching, use the curriculum materials your leader directs you to use.
- Prepare each lesson thoroughly and prayerfully.
- Try to attend every teachers' meeting, to help plan unit projects, set up goals, share problems and prayer needs, and contribute constructive ideas.
- Think of your class as an important part of the entire department, not as your own little group on which to try out pet theories or doctrines.
- Enthusiastically support department contests and projects, encouraging your class to take part, and working with them, even on a weeknight or Saturday at times.
- Fit your class socials into the department plan for get-togethers, avoiding conflicts and misunderstandings.
- Faithfully follow up absentees and turn in reports on them to the department secretary.
- Be a dependable year-round teacher.
- Be patient with your leader's shortcomings (if he has some), and talk to God about them. He needs your faithful prayer support.

Make it yours

1. What three steps will help make your assembly time worthwhile, if it is not now?
2. Plan to talk with your departmental leader this week about making Sunday School a more effective joint ministry.

Reaching into the home
8

It was Barb's 14th birthday. As she left for school that morning, her
mom told her, "We're going to have a special guest for dinner this
evening." Despite her daughter's pleas, she wouldn't reveal the secret.
So the excited teenager wondered throughout the day who the special
person would be.

That evening she was surprised and delighted. The "mystery" guest
was her young Sunday School teacher who had left the area shortly
after she had been married. Now she had returned to visit friends, and
was proudly showing them her two-month-old son.

For an entire evening the teacher joined in the happiness of the
birthday celebration, also sharing the joy that God had given her in
the blessings of Christian marriage and motherhood. Her visit was a
continuation of the relationship she had begun with the teenager and
her family two years earlier. Throughout those years she had opened
her life to a small class of junior high girls, letting them in on the
activities she was experiencing on a college campus, as well as sharing
with them some of the problems she faced. Her hopes and dreams for
future years became the hopes and dreams of her girls for her. She
took them on camping trips, cheered for them at their school sports
events, prayed with them about family concerns, and taught them to
spend "a little time with Jesus" alone each day.

What was this young woman's understanding of what it means to be a Sunday School teacher? What is yours?

Students and their families need tender loving care

To be as effective as God wants it to be, your teaching must extend beyond your classroom walls. You have to let your students into your world, and you must be willing to enter into theirs. Some of the kids you face each week come from broken homes, or homes in which there is constant arguing and fighting. Some are struggling to adapt to living with stepmothers or stepfathers, or with older grandparents in the home. Some may be living with only one parent. Others may be facing psychological or physical abuse. They need the healing and comfort that Christ can bring, through the love and care you show them.

Here are ways you can minister to teens and their families:

1. Think of each teen as a friend. Greet him and talk with him as you would an adult friend. Whenever you see him at church or other functions, take time to spend a few minutes in conversation with him.

2. Mark on your calendar some days you will do something special with each person in your group. This may be as simple as having a Coke and hamburger with him at a nearby restaurant. What is important is spending time alone with him, finding out his likes and dislikes, problems, and feelings. Most important is taking the time to *listen*. Maybe you're the only adult who will.

3. Visit the home of each young teen early in the year so you will know the kind of place where he spends most of his life. Be observant, and take a sincere interest in what is happening there. Show genuine warmth and understanding toward the parents.

4. Start a small loose-leaf notebook, with a page for the family of each student. Record birth dates, graduations, retirements, planned hospital stays, and phone numbers—anything you want to remember about the families that you care about. Use the notebook for handy reference and also as a prayer reminder.

5. Call your teens and their families often on the phone. Tell the parents what you genuinely appreciate about their kids, and show an interest in current happenings in their homes.

6. Hold an open house for parents in the Sunday School department. Let them in on what you and your students are studying, and show them any projects you are making. If there are ways parents can help you, invite them to lend their expertise.

7. From time to time, open your classroom for parents to come and observe, share testimonies, or tell prayer requests.

8. Call on parents for help with socials, transportation, or special events. Let them know that you consider your ministry a joint one with them.

9. Use the parents as valuable resources in finding out helpful information about their young people. They will probably enjoy telling you about their kids' hobbies and abilities, interests, reading preferences, friendships, and academic areas that need improvement.

10. If possible, invite parents into your home from time to time. Let them see you in a setting other than at church. Build friendships with them, and as the Lord leads and opens opportunities, invite unchurched parents to church and other Christian functions. Above all, pray that the Lord will use you as a godly influence in the families of your teens, and help you develop lasting relationships with them.

Make it yours

1. Start now to build a file on interesting information about the family of each of your teens.

2. Today, call at least one person in your class and show an interest in what's happening in his family.

3. Think of something your teens can do to let their families know how much they mean to them. Work on this project as a class, letting teens take the initiative in carrying it out.

4. Think about what it means to "disciple" a young teen for Christ. Do you have this kind of relationship with any young person in your class? What does your discipling a young person have to do with your association with his family?

5. With your departmental leader and other teachers, begin now to plan a Parents' Day for your junior high department. How will you involve your teens?

Additional resources

Blos, Peter. *The Young Adolescent.* New York: The Free Press, 1970.

Brown, Paul. *Teaching Junior Hi's and Senior Hi's.* Cincinnati, Ohio: Standard Publishing Company.

Browning, Robert. *Communicating with Junior Highs.* Nashville, Tenn.: Graded Press, 1968.

Burton, Janet. *Guiding Youth.* Nashville, Tenn.: Convention Press.

Darkes, Anna Sue. *How to Make Transparencies Simply and Economically.* Lititz, Pa.: Faith Venture Visuals, Inc.

Dobson, James. *Preparing for Adolescence.* Santa Ana, Calif.: Vision House, 1978.

Frans, Mike. *Are Junior Highs MISSING PERSONS From Your Youth Ministry?* Wheaton, Ill.: Victor Books, 1979.

Getz, Gene. *Audio-Visual Media in Christian Education.* Chicago, Ill.: Moody Press.

Holderness, Ginny Ward. *The Exuberant Years.* Atlanta: John Knox Press, 1976.

Johnson, Eric W. *How to Live Through Junior High School.* Philadelphia and New York: J. B. Lippincott Co., 1975.

Kagan, Jerome and Coles, Robert, Editors. *Early Adolescence.* New York: W. W. Norton, 1972.

LeFever, Marlene D. *Turnabout Teaching.* D. C. Cook Publishing Co., Elgin, Ill., 1973.

Lipsitz, Joan. *Growing Up Forgotten.* Lexington, Ma.: Lexington Books, 1977.

Mayle, Peter. *What's Happening To Me? A Guide to Puberty.* Secacus, N. J.: Lyle Stuart, Inc., 1975.

McCasland, David. *From SWAMP To SOLID GROUND Teaching Junior Highs Successfully.* Wheaton, Ill.: Victor Books, 1980.

Minor and Frye. *Techniques for Producing Instructional Media.* New York: McGraw-Hill Publishing Co.

Minton, Lynn. *Growing Into Adolescence.* New York: Parent's Press, 1972.

Reichert, Fr. Richards. "Prime Time" (two cassettes on junior high ministry) N.C.R. Cassettes, P.O. Box 281, Kansas City, Mo. 64141.

Rice, Wayne. *Junior High Ministry.* Grand Rapids: Zondervan, 1978.

Richards, Lawrence O. *Creative Bible Teaching.* Chicago, Ill.: Moody Press.

Richards, Lawrence O. *You and Teaching.* Chicago, Ill.: Moody Press.

Zuck, Roy B. *Spiritual Power in Your Teaching.* Chicago, Ill.: Moody Press.

Curriculums

Corbett, Janice M. *Explore: Resources for Junior Highs in the Church.* Valley Forge, Pa.: Judson Press, 1978.

McAllister, Dawson, and Webster, Dan. *Discussion Manual for Student Relationships*—Volumes I and II. Glendale, Calif.: Shepherd Productions, Inc., 1975.

Scripture Press All-Bible Curriculum for Young Teens, Wheaton, Ill.